Step-by-Step, Practical Recipes Baking Br[eads]

Everyday Breads

For simple, everyday loaves of bread and bread rolls, choose from the delicious list of recipes below.

A Tasty Difference

More interesting styles of bread make family meals go a long way, and are sometimes almost a meal in themselves.

Sweet Bakes

Simple ingredients, combined in classic cake recipes, make for truly scrumptious results that no one will be able to resist.

FLAME TREE RECIPE BOOKS

FLAME TREE has been creating family-friendly, classic and beginner recipes for our bestselling cookbooks for over 12 years now. Our mission is to offer you a wide range of expert-tested dishes, while providing clear images of the final dish so that you can match it to your own results. We hope you enjoy this super selection of recipes – there are plenty more to try! Titles in this series include:

Cupcakes • Slow Cooker • Curries Chinese • Soups • Baking Breads Cakes • Simple Suppers • Pasta Chicken • Fish & Seafood • Chocolate

For more information please visit:
www.flametreepublishing.com

Rustic Country Bread

INGREDIENTS

Makes 1 large loaf

Sourdough starter:
225 g/8 oz strong white flour
2 tsp easy-blend dried yeast
300 ml/ ½ pint warm water

Bread dough:
350 g/12 oz strong white flour
25 g/1 oz rye flour
1½ tsp salt
½ tsp caster sugar
1 tsp dried yeast
1 tsp sunflower oil
175 ml/6 fl oz warm water

To finish:
2 tsp plain flour
2 tsp rye flour

HELPFUL HINT
Put the remaining starter in a pan, stir in 125 ml/4 fl oz of warm water and 125 g/4 oz strong white flour. Stir twice a day for 2–3 days and use as a starter for another loaf.

1 Preheat the oven to 220°C/425°F/Gas Mark 7, 15 minutes before baking. For the starter, sift the flour into a bowl. Stir in the yeast and make a well in the centre. Pour in the warm water and mix with a fork.

2 Transfer to a saucepan, cover with a clean tea towel and leave for 2–3 days at room temperature. Stir the mixture and spray with a little water twice a day.

3 For the dough, mix the flours, salt, sugar and yeast in a bowl. Add 225 ml/8 fl oz of the starter, the oil and the warm water. Mix to a soft dough.

4 Knead on a lightly floured surface for 10 minutes until smooth and elastic. Put in an oiled bowl, cover and leave to rise in a warm place for about 1½ hours, or until doubled in size.

5 Turn the dough out and knead for a minute or two. Shape into a round loaf and place on an oiled baking sheet.

6 Cover with oiled clingfilm and leave to rise for 1 hour, or until doubled in size.

7 Dust the loaf with flour, then using a sharp knife make several slashes across the top of the loaf. Slash across the loaf in the opposite direction to make a square pattern.

8 Bake in the preheated oven for 40–45 minutes, or until golden brown and hollow-sounding when tapped underneath. Cool on a wire rack and serve.

2   6   7

Mixed Grain Bread

INGREDIENTS

Makes 1 large loaf

350 g/12 oz strong white flour

2 tsp salt

225 g/8 oz strong Granary flour

125 g/4 oz rye flour

25 g/1 oz butter, diced

2 tsp easy-blend dried yeast

25 g/1 oz rolled oats

2 tbsp sunflower seeds

1 tbsp malt extract

450 ml/ ³/₄ pint warm water (see
  Helpful Hint)

1 medium egg, beaten

HELPFUL HINT

The amount of water you need to add to the dry ingredients in this recipe will depend on the type and brand of flour you use. Add just enough water to make a soft elastic dough.

1 Preheat the oven to 220°C/425°F/Gas Mark 7, 15 minutes before baking. Sift the white flour and salt into a large bowl. Stir in the Granary and rye flours, then rub in the butter until the mixture resembles breadcrumbs. Stir in the yeast, oats and seeds and make a well in the centre.

2 Stir the malt extract into the warm water until dissolved. Add the malt water to the dry ingredients. Mix to a soft dough.

3 Turn the dough out on to a lightly floured surface and knead for 10 minutes, until smooth and elastic.

4 Put in an oiled bowl, cover with clingfilm and leave to rise in a warm place for 1¹/₂ hours or until doubled in size.

5 Turn out and knead again for a minute or two to knock out the air.

6 Shape into an oval loaf about 30.5 cm/12 inches long and place on a well-oiled baking sheet.

7 Cover with oiled clingfilm and leave to rise for 40 minutes, or until doubled in size.

8 Brush the loaf with beaten egg and bake in the preheated oven for 35–45 minutes, or until the bread is well risen, browned and sounds hollow when the base is tapped. Leave to cool on a wire rack, then serve.

2

4

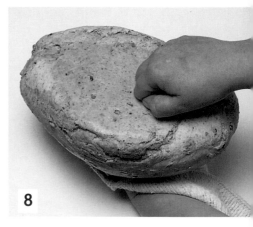

8

Classic White Loaf

INGREDIENTS

Makes 1 x 900 g/ 2 lb loaf

700 g/1½ lb strong white flour
1 tbsp salt
25 g/1 oz butter, cubed
1 tsp caster sugar
2 tsp easy-blend dried yeast
150 ml/ ¼ pint milk
300 ml/ ½ pint warm water
1 tbsp plain flour, to dredge

Light wholemeal variation:

450 g/1 lb strong wholemeal flour
225 g/8 oz strong white flour
beaten egg, to glaze
1 tbsp kibbled wheat, to finish

1 Preheat the oven to 220°C/425°F/Gas Mark 7, 15 minutes before baking. Oil and line the base of a 900 g/2 lb loaf tin with greaseproof paper. Sift the flour and salt into a large bowl. Rub in the butter, then stir in the sugar and yeast. Make a well in the centre.

2 Add the milk and the warm water to the dry ingredients. Mix to a soft dough, adding a little more water if needed. Turn out the dough and knead on a lightly floured surface for 10 minutes, or until smooth and elastic.

3 Place the dough in an oiled bowl, cover with clingfilm or a clean tea towel and leave in a warm place to rise for 1 hour, or until doubled in size. Knead again for a minute or two to knock out the air.

4 Shape the dough into an oblong and place in the prepared tin. Cover with oiled clingfilm and leave to rise for a further 30 minutes or until the dough reaches the top of the tin. Dredge the top of the loaf with flour or brush with the egg glaze and scatter with kibbled wheat if making the wholemeal version. Bake the loaf on the middle shelf of the preheated oven for 15 minutes.

5 Turn down the oven to 200°C/400°F/Gas Mark 6. Bake the loaf for a further 20–25 minutes, or until well risen and hollow sounding when tapped underneath. Turn out, cool on a wire rack and serve.

TASTY TIP

Nothing beats a freshly-cooked loaf of white bread. While the bread is still warm, spread generously with fresh butter and eat.

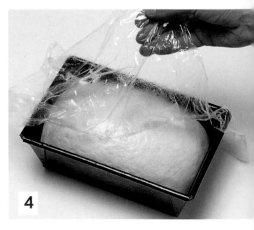

Quick Brown Bread

INGREDIENTS

Makes 2 x 450 g/ 1 lb loaves

700 g/1½ lb strong wholemeal flour
2 tsp salt
½ tsp caster sugar
7 g/ ¼ oz sachet easy-blend dried yeast
450 ml/ ¾ pint warm water

To finish:

beaten egg, to glaze
1 tbsp plain white flour, to dust

Onion & caraway seed rolls:

1 small onion, peeled and
   finely chopped
1 tbsp olive oil
2 tbsp caraway seeds
milk, to glaze

HELPFUL HINT

For most breads the dough is kneaded, left to rise, kneaded, shaped and then left to rise again. This bread does not need the first rising – simply knead, shape, rise and bake.

1 Preheat the oven to 200°C/400°F/Gas Mark 6, 15 minutes before baking. Oil two 450 g/1 lb loaf tins. Sift the flour, salt and sugar into a large bowl, adding the remaining bran in the sieve. Stir in the yeast, then make a well in the centre.

2 Pour the warm water into the dry ingredients and mix to form a soft dough, adding a little more water if needed.

3 Knead on a lightly floured surface for 10 minutes, until smooth and elastic.

4 Divide in half, shape into two oblongs and place in the tins. Cover with oiled clingfilm and leave in a warm place for 40 minutes, or until risen to the top of the tins.

5 Glaze one loaf with the beaten egg and dust the other loaf generously with the plain flour.

6 Bake the loaves in the preheated oven for 35 minutes or until well risen and lightly browned. Turn out of the tins and return to the oven for 5 minutes to crisp the sides. Cool on a wire rack.

7 For the onion and caraway seed rolls, gently fry the onion in the oil until soft. Reserve until the onions are cool, then stir into the dry ingredients with 1 tablespoon of the caraway seeds. Make the dough as before.

8 Divide the dough into 16 pieces and shape into rolls. Put on two oiled baking trays, cover with oiled clingfilm and prove for 30 minutes.

9 Glaze the rolls with milk and sprinkle with the rest of the seeds. Bake for 25–30 minutes, cool on a wire rack and serve.

1

4

5

Soft Dinner Rolls

INGREDIENTS

Makes 16

50 g/2 oz butter
1 tbsp caster sugar
225 ml/8 fl oz milk
550 g/1¼ lbs strong white flour
1½ tsp salt
2 tsp easy-blend dried yeast
2 medium eggs, beaten

To glaze & finish:

2 tbsp milk
1 tsp sea salt
2 tsp poppy seeds

HELPFUL HINT

For clover leaf rolls, divide into three equal pieces and roll each into a ball. Place the balls together in a triangular shape. For cottage buns, divide the dough into two-thirds and one-third pieces. Shape each piece into a round, then put the smaller one on top of the larger one. Push a floured wooden spoon handle or finger through the middle of the top one and into the bottom one to join together.

1 Preheat the oven to 220°C/425°F/Gas Mark 7, 15 minutes before baking. Gently heat the butter, sugar and milk in a saucepan until the butter has melted and the sugar has dissolved. Cool until tepid. Sift the flour and salt into a bowl, stir in the yeast and make a well in the centre. Reserve 1 tablespoon of the beaten eggs. Add the rest to the dry ingredients with the milk mixture. Mix to form a soft dough.

2 Knead the dough on a lightly floured surface for 10 minutes until smooth and elastic. Put in an oiled bowl, cover with clingfilm and leave in a warm place to rise for 1 hour, or until doubled in size. Knead again for a minute or two, then divide into 16 pieces. Shape into plaits, snails, clover leaves and cottage buns (see Helpful Hints). Place on two oiled baking sheets, cover with oiled clingfilm and leave to rise for 30 minutes, until doubled in size.

3 Mix the reserved beaten egg with the milk and brush over the rolls. Sprinkle some with sea salt, others with poppy seeds and leave some plain. Bake in the preheated oven for about 20 minutes, or until golden and hollow sounding when tapped underneath. Transfer to a wire rack. Cover with a clean tea towel while cooling to keep the rolls soft and serve.

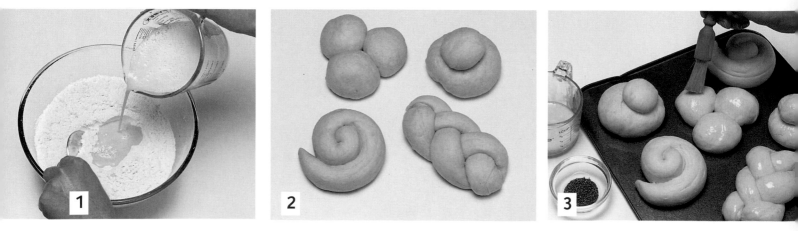

Bagels

INGREDIENTS

Serves 4

450 g/1 lb strong plain flour
1½ tsp salt
2 tsp easy-blend dried yeast
2 medium eggs
1 tsp clear honey
2 tbsp sunflower oil
250 ml/9 fl oz tepid water

To finish:

1 tbsp caster sugar
beaten egg, to glaze
2 tsp poppy seeds
½ small onion, peeled and finely
   chopped
2 tsp sunflower oil

TASTY TIP

Why not try bagels for breakfast? They are delicious filled with cheese and ham or served toasted with scrambled egg. They are also good with smoked salmon and cream cheese.

1 Preheat the oven to 200°C/400°F/Gas Mark 6, 15 minutes before baking. Sift the flour and salt into a large bowl. Stir in the yeast, then make a well in the centre. Whisk the eggs together with the honey and oil. Add to the dry ingredients with the tepid water and mix to form a soft dough.

2 Knead the dough on a lightly floured surface for 10 minutes until smooth and elastic. Put in a bowl, cover with clingfilm and leave in a warm place to rise for 45 minutes, or until doubled in size.

3 Briefly knead the dough again to knock out the air. Divide into 12 pieces, form each into a 20.5 cm/8 inch roll, curve into a ring and pinch the edges to seal.

4 Put the rings on an oiled baking sheet, cover with oiled clingfilm and leave to rise in a warm place for 20 minutes, or until risen and puffy.

5 Add the caster sugar to a large saucepan of water. Bring to the boil, then drop in the bagels, one at a time and poach for 15 seconds. Lift out with a slotted spoon and return to the baking tray.

6 Brush the bagels with beaten egg and sprinkle one-third with poppy seeds. Mix together the onion and oil and sprinkle over another third of the bagels. Leave the remaining third plain.

7 Bake in the preheated oven for 12–15 minutes, or until golden brown. Transfer to a wire rack and serve when cool.

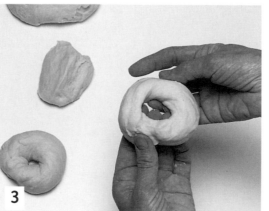

Sweet Potato Baps

INGREDIENTS

Makes 16

225 g/8 oz sweet potato
15 g/ ½ oz butter
freshly grated nutmeg
about 200 ml/7 fl oz milk
450 g/1 lb strong white flour
2 tsp salt
7 g/ ¼ oz sachet easy-blend yeast
1 medium egg, beaten

To finish:

beaten egg, to glaze
1 tbsp rolled oats

HELPFUL HINT

There are many varieties of sweet potato, so be sure to choose the correct potato for this recipe, as their flavours and textures vary. The sweet potato used in this recipe is dark skinned and has a vibrant orange flesh which cooks to a moist texture.

1 Preheat the oven to 200°C/400°F/Gas Mark 6, 15 minutes before baking. Peel the sweet potato and cut into large chunks. Cook in a saucepan of boiling water for 12–15 minutes, or until tender.

2 Drain well and mash with the butter and nutmeg. Stir in the milk, then leave until barely warm.

3 Sift the flour and salt into a large bowl. Stir in the yeast. Make a well in the centre.

4 Add the mashed sweet potato and beaten egg and mix to a soft dough. Add a little more milk if needed, depending on the moisture in the sweet potato.

5 Turn out the dough on to a lightly floured surface and knead for about 10 minutes, or until smooth and elastic. Place in a lightly oiled bowl, cover with clingfilm and leave in a warm place to rise for about 1 hour, or until the dough doubles in size.

6 Turn out the dough and knead for a minute or two until smooth. Divide into 16 pieces, shape into rolls and place on a large oiled baking sheet. Cover with oiled clingfilm and leave to rise for 15 minutes.

7 Brush the rolls with beaten egg, then sprinkle half with rolled oats and leave the rest plain.

8 Bake in the preheated oven for 12–15 minutes, or until the rolls are well risen, lightly browned and sound hollow when the bases are tapped. Transfer to a wire rack and immediately cover with a clean tea towel to keep the crusts soft.

4

6

8

Rosemary & Olive Focaccia

INGREDIENTS

Makes 2 loaves

700 g/1½ lb strong white flour
pinch of salt
pinch of caster sugar
7 g/ ¼ oz sachet easy-blend dried yeast
2 tsp freshly chopped rosemary
450 ml/ ¾ pint warm water
3 tbsp olive oil
75 g/3 oz pitted black olives,
  roughly chopped
sprigs of rosemary, to garnish

To finish:
3 tbsp olive oil
coarse sea salt
freshly ground black pepper

TASTY TIP

You could replace the rosemary with some chopped sun-dried tomatoes. Knead the tomatoes into the dough along with the olives in step 3, then, before baking, drizzle with the oil and replace the salt with some grated mozzarella cheese.

1 Preheat the oven to 200°C/400°F/Gas Mark 6, 15 minutes before baking. Sift the flour, salt and sugar into a large bowl. Stir in the yeast and rosemary. Make a well in the centre.

2 Pour in the warm water and the oil and mix to a soft dough. Turn out on to a lightly floured surface and knead for about 10 minutes, until smooth and elastic.

3 Pat the olives dry on kitchen paper, then gently knead into the dough. Put in an oiled bowl, cover with clingfilm and leave to rise in a warm place for 1½ hours, or until it has doubled in size.

4 Turn out the dough and knead again for a minute or two. Divide in half and roll out each piece to a 25.5 cm/10 inch circle.

5 Transfer to oiled baking sheets, cover with oiled clingfilm and leave to rise for 30 minutes.

6 Using the fingertips, make deep dimples all over the dough. Drizzle with the oil and sprinkle with sea salt.

7 Bake in the preheated oven for 20–25 minutes, or until risen and golden. Cool on a wire rack and garnish with sprigs of rosemary. Grind over a little black pepper before serving.

3

4

6

Daktyla-style Bread

INGREDIENTS

Makes 1 loaf

350 g/12 oz strong white flour
125 g/4 oz wholemeal flour
1 tsp salt
50 g/2 oz fine cornmeal
2 tsp easy-blend dried yeast
2 tsp clear honey
1 tbsp olive oil
4 tbsp milk
250 ml/9 fl oz water

To glaze & finish:
4 tbsp milk
4 tbsp sesame seeds

FOOD FACT
Daktyla was traditionally made in Cyprus during Lent. The Cypriots made crisp, syrup-soaked fingers of pastry filled with an almond and cinnamon filling. In this recipe the bread is shaped into oblongs and baked so that the bread can be broken into fingers to eat.

1 Preheat the oven to 220°C/425°F/Gas Mark 7, 15 minutes before baking. Sift the white and wholemeal flours and salt into a large bowl, adding the bran left in the sieve. Stir in the cornmeal and yeast. Make a well in the centre.

2 Put the honey, oil, milk and water in a saucepan and heat gently until tepid. Add to the dry ingredients and mix to a soft dough, adding a little more water if needed.

3 Knead the dough on a lightly floured surface for 10 minutes, until smooth and elastic. Put in an oiled bowl, cover with clingfilm and leave to rise in a warm place for 1½ hours or until it has doubled in size.

4 Turn the dough out and knead for a minute or two. Shape into a long oval about 25.5 cm/10 inches long. Cut the oval into six equal pieces. Shape each piece into an oblong, then on an oiled baking sheet arrange in a row so that all the pieces of dough are touching.

5 Cover with oiled clingfilm and leave for 45 minutes, or until doubled in size.

6 Brush the bread with milk, then scatter with sesame seeds.

7 Bake the bread in the preheated oven for 40–45 minutes, or until golden brown and hollow-sounding when tapped underneath. Cool on a wire rack and serve.

3

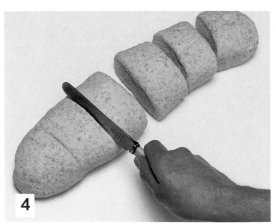
4

6

Spicy Filled Naan Bread

INGREDIENTS

Makes 6

400 g/14 oz strong white flour
1 tsp salt
1 tsp easy-blend dried yeast
15 g/ ½ oz ghee or unsalted
   butter, melted
1 tsp clear honey
200 ml/7 fl oz warm water

For the filling:

25 g/1 oz ghee or unsalted butter
1 small onion, peeled and finely
   chopped
1 garlic clove, peeled and crushed
1 tsp ground coriander
1 tsp ground cumin
2 tsp grated fresh root ginger
pinch of chilli powder
pinch of ground cinnamon
salt and freshly ground black pepper

HELPFUL HINT

Ghee is more expensive than other butters but it has a longer life and a much higher smoke point (190°C/375°F). Ghee, therefore, is practical for sautéing and frying.

1 Preheat the oven to 220°C/450°F/Gas Mark 8, 15 minutes before baking and place a large baking sheet in it to heat up. Sift the flour and salt into a large bowl. Stir in the yeast and make a well in the centre. Add the ghee or melted butter, honey and the warm water. Mix to a soft dough.

2 Knead the dough on a lightly floured surface, until smooth and elastic. Put in a lightly oiled bowl, cover with clingfilm and leave to rise for 1 hour, or until doubled in size.

3 For the filling, melt the ghee or butter in a frying pan and gently cook the onion for about 5 minutes. Stir in the garlic and spices and season to taste with salt and pepper. Cook for a further 6–7 minutes, until soft. Remove from the heat, stir in 1 tablespoon of water and leave to cool.

4 Briefly knead the dough, then divide into six pieces. Roll out each piece of dough to 12.5 cm/5 inch rounds. Spoon the filling on to one half of each round.

5 Fold over and press the edges together to seal. Re-roll to shape into flat ovals, about 16 cm/6½ inches long.

6 Cover with oiled clingfilm and leave to rise for about 15 minutes.

7 Transfer the breads to the hot baking sheet and cook in the preheated oven for 10–12 minutes, until puffed up and lightly browned. Serve hot.

3

4

5

Irish Soda Bread

INGREDIENTS

Makes 1 loaf

400 g/14 oz plain white flour,
   plus 1 tbsp for dusting
1 tsp salt
2 tsp bicarbonate of soda
15 g/ ½ oz butter
50 g/2 oz coarse oatmeal
1 tsp clear honey
300 ml/ ½ pint buttermilk
2 tbsp milk

Wholemeal variation:

400 g/14 oz plain wholemeal flour,
   plus 1 tbsp, to dust
1 tbsp milk

TASTY TIP

Soda bread relies on the raising agent bicarbonate of soda, which when combined with the acidic buttermilk enables the bread to rise. For an unusual Irish soda bread, knead in a handful of currants and 2 tablespoons of caraway seeds in step 3. According to Irish tradition, the cross on the top of the bread is intended to scare away the devil.

1 Preheat the oven to 200°C/400°F/Gas Mark 6, 15 minutes before baking. Sift the flour, salt and bicarbonate of soda into a large bowl. Rub in the butter until the mixture resembles fine breadcrumbs. Stir in the oatmeal and make a well in the centre.

2 Mix the honey, buttermilk and milk together and add to the dry ingredients. Mix to a soft dough.

3 Knead the dough on a lightly floured surface for 2–3 minutes, until the dough is smooth. Shape into a 20.5 cm/8 inch round and place on an oiled baking sheet.

4 Thickly dust the top of the bread with flour. Using a sharp knife, cut a deep cross on top, going about halfway through the loaf.

5 Bake in the preheated oven on the middle shelf of the oven for 30–35 minutes or until the bread is slightly risen, golden and sounds hollow when tapped underneath. Cool on a wire rack. Eat on the day of making.

6 For a wholemeal soda bread, use all the wholemeal flour instead of the white flour and add an extra tablespoon of milk when mixing together. Dust the top with wholemeal flour and bake.

Fruited Brioche Buns

INGREDIENTS

Makes 12

225 g/8 oz strong white flour
pinch of salt
1 tbsp caster sugar
7 g/ ¼ oz sachet easy-blend dried yeast
2 large eggs, beaten
50 g/2 oz butter, melted
beaten egg, to glaze

For the filling:

40 g/1½ oz blanched
  almonds, chopped
50 g/2 oz luxury mixed dried fruit
1 tsp light soft brown sugar
2 tsp orange liqueur or brandy

1 Preheat the oven to 220°C/425°F/Gas Mark 7, 15 minutes before baking. Sift the flour and salt into a bowl. Stir in the sugar and yeast. Make a well in the centre. Add the eggs, butter and 2 tablespoons of warm water and mix to a soft dough.

2 Knead the dough on a lightly floured surface for 5 minutes, until smooth and elastic. Put in an oiled bowl, cover with clingfilm and leave to rise in a warm place for 1 hour, or until it has doubled in size.

3 Mix the ingredients for the filling together, cover the bowl and leave to soak while the dough is rising.

4 Re-knead the dough for a minute or two, then divide into 12 pieces. Take 1 piece at a time and flatten three-quarters into a 6.5 cm/2½ inch round. Spoon a little filling in the centre, then pinch the edges together to enclose. Put seam-side down into a well-greased fluted 12-hole bun tin.

5 Shape the smaller piece of dough into a round and place on top of the larger one.

6 Push a finger or floured wooden spoon handle through the middle of the top one and into the bottom one to join them together. Repeat with the remaining balls of dough.

7 Cover the brioche with oiled clingfilm and leave for about 20 minutes, or until well risen.

8 Brush the brioches with beaten egg and bake in the preheated oven for 10–12 minutes, or until golden. Cool on a wire rack and serve.

3

4

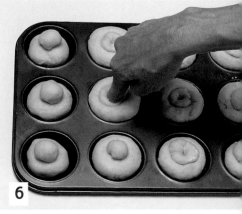

6

Bacon & Tomato Breakfast Twist

INGREDIENTS

Serves 8

450 g/1 lb strong plain flour
½ tsp salt
7 g/ ¼ oz sachet easy-blend dried yeast
300 ml/ ½ pint warm milk
15 g/ ½ oz butter, melted

For the filling:

225 g/8 oz back bacon, derinded
15 g/ ½ oz butter, melted
175 g/6 oz ripe tomatoes, peeled,
   deseeded and chopped
freshly ground black pepper

To finish:

beaten egg, to glaze
2 tsp medium oatmeal

1 Preheat the oven to 200°C/400°F/Gas Mark 6, 15 minutes before baking. Sift the flour and salt into a large bowl. Stir in the yeast and make a well in the centre. Pour in the milk and butter and mix to a soft dough.

2 Knead on a lightly floured surface for 10 minutes, until smooth and elastic. Put in an oiled bowl, cover with clingfilm and leave to rise in a warm place for 1 hour, until doubled in size.

3 Cook the bacon under a hot grill for 5–6 minutes, turning once until crisp. Leave to cool, then roughly chop.

4 Knead the dough again for a minute or two. Roll it out to a 25.5 x 33 cm/10 x 13 inch rectangle. Cut in half lengthways. Lightly brush with butter, then scatter with the bacon, tomatoes and black pepper, leaving a 1 cm/½ inch margin around the edges.

5 Brush the edges of the dough with beaten egg, then roll up each rectangle lengthways.

6 Place the two rolls side by side and twist together, pinching the ends to seal.

7 Transfer to an oiled baking sheet and loosely cover with oiled clingfilm. Leave to rise in a warm place for 30 minutes.

8 Brush with the beaten egg and sprinkle with the oatmeal. Bake in the preheated oven for about 30 minutes, or until golden brown and hollow-sounding when tapped on the base. Serve the bread warm in thick slices.

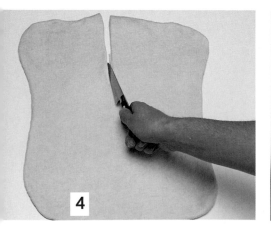

4

5

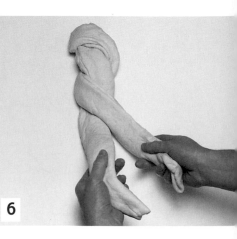

6

Traditional Oven Scones

INGREDIENTS

Makes 8

225 g/8 oz self-raising flour
1 tsp baking powder
pinch of salt
40 g/1½ oz butter, cubed
15 g/ ½ oz caster sugar
150 ml/ ¼ pint milk, plus 1 tbsp
   for brushing
1 tbsp plain flour, to dust

Lemon & sultana scone variation:

50 g/2 oz sultanas
finely grated rind of ½ lemon
beaten egg, to glaze

1 Preheat the oven to 220°C/425°F/Gas Mark 7, 15 minutes before baking. Sift the flour, baking powder and salt into a large bowl. Rub in the butter until the mixture resembles fine breadcrumbs. Stir in the sugar and mix in enough milk to give a fairly soft dough.

2 Knead the dough on a lightly floured surface for a few seconds until smooth. Roll out until 2 cm/¾ inches thick and stamp out 6.5 cm/2½ inch rounds with a floured plain cutter.

3 Place on an oiled baking sheet and brush the tops with milk – do not brush it over the sides or the scones will not rise properly. Dust with a little plain flour.

4 Bake in the preheated oven for 12–15 minutes, or until well risen and golden brown. Transfer to a wire rack and serve warm or leave to cool completely. The scones are best eaten on the day of baking but may be kept in an airtight tin for up to 2 days.

5 For lemon and sultana scones, stir in the sultanas and lemon rind with the sugar. Roll out until 2 cm/¾ inches thick and cut into eight fingers, 10 x 2.5 cm/4 x 1 inch in size. Bake the scones as before.

TASTY TIP

Nothing beats scones still warm from the oven. Split the scones open and fill with a layer of juicy strawberry jam and clotted cream. Serve the scones with a pot of Earl Grey tea for a delicious afternoon treat.

Cheese-crusted Potato Scones

INGREDIENTS

Makes 6

200 g/7 oz self-raising flour
25 g/1 oz wholemeal flour
½ tsp salt
1½ tsp baking powder
25 g/1 oz butter, cubed
5 tbsp milk
175 g/6 oz cold mashed potato
freshly ground black pepper

To finish:

2 tbsp milk
40 g/1½ oz mature Cheddar cheese,
  finely grated
paprika pepper, to dust
sprig of basil, to garnish

1 Preheat the oven to 220°C/425°F/Gas Mark 7, 15 minutes before baking. Sift the flours, salt and baking powder into a large bowl. Rub in the butter until the mixture resembles fine breadcrumbs.

2 Stir 4 tablespoons of the milk into the mashed potato and season with black pepper.

3 Add the dry ingredients to the potato mixture, mixing together with a fork and adding the remaining 1 tablespoon of milk if needed.

4 Knead the dough on a lightly floured surface for a few seconds until smooth. Roll out to a 15 cm/6 inch round and transfer to an oiled baking sheet.

5 Mark the scone round into six wedges, cutting about halfway through with a small sharp knife.

6 Brush with milk, then sprinkle with the cheese and a faint dusting of paprika.

7 Bake on the middle shelf of the preheated oven for 15 minutes, or until well risen and golden brown.

8 Transfer to a wire rack and leave to cool for 5 minutes before breaking into wedges.

9 Serve warm or leave to cool completely. Once cool, store the scones in an airtight tin. Garnish with a sprig of basil and serve split and buttered.

FOOD FACT

The scone supposedly acquired its name from the Stone of Destiny (or Scone) in Scotland, where Scottish Kings were once crowned.

2

5

6

Lemon & Ginger Buns

INGREDIENTS

Makes 15

175 g/6 oz butter or margarine
350 g/12 oz plain flour
2 tsp baking powder
½ tsp ground ginger
pinch of salt
finely grated rind of 1 lemon
175 g/6 oz soft light brown sugar
125 g/4 oz sultanas
75 g/3 oz chopped mixed peel
25 g/1 oz stem ginger, finely chopped
1 medium egg
juice of 1 lemon

TASTY TIP

For a gooey, sticky treat, brush the buns with a little syrup from the jar of stem ginger, and scatter with some extra finely chopped stem ginger as soon as they have been removed from the oven.

1 Preheat the oven to 220°C/425°F/Gas Mark 7, 15 minutes before baking. Cut the butter or margarine into small pieces and place in a large bowl.

2 Sift the flour, baking powder, ginger and salt together and add to the butter with the lemon rind.

3 Using the fingertips, rub the butter into the flour and spice mixture until it resembles coarse breadcrumbs.

4 Stir in the sugar, sultanas, chopped mixed peel and stem ginger.

5 Add the egg and lemon juice to the mixture, then using a round bladed knife stir well to mix. The mixture should be quite stiff and just holding together.

6 Place heaped tablespoons of the mixture on to a lightly oiled baking tray, making sure that the dollops of mixture are well apart.

7 Using a fork, rough up the edges of the buns and bake in the preheated oven for 12–15 minutes.

8 Leave the buns to cool for 5 minutes before transferring to a wire rack until cold, then serve. Otherwise store the buns in an airtight tin and eat within 3–5 days.

3

5

7

Jammy Buns

INGREDIENTS

Makes 12

175 g/6 oz plain flour
175 g/6 oz wholemeal flour
2 tsp baking powder
150 g/5 oz butter or margarine
125 g/4 oz golden caster sugar
50 g/2 oz dried cranberries
1 large egg, beaten
1 tbsp milk
4–5 tbsp seedless raspberry jam

TASTY TIP

In this recipe, any type of jam can be used. However, look for one with a high fruit content. Alternatively replace the jam with a fruit compote. Simply boil some fruit with a little sugar and water, then leave to cool before placing inside the buns.

1 Preheat the oven to 190°C/375°F/Gas Mark 5, 10 minutes before baking. Lightly oil a large baking sheet.

2 Sift the flours and baking powder together into a large bowl, then tip in the grains remaining in the sieve.

3 Cut the butter or margarine into small pieces. It is easier to do this when the butter is in the flour as it helps stop the butter from sticking to the knife.

4 Rub the butter into the flours until it resembles coarse breadcrumbs. Stir in the sugar and cranberries.

5 Using a round bladed knife, stir in the beaten egg and milk. Mix to form a firm dough. Divide the mixture into 12 and roll into balls.

6 Place the dough balls on the baking tray, leaving enough space for expansion. Press the thumb into the centre of each ball making a small hollow.

7 Spoon a little of the jam in each hollow. Pinch lightly to seal the tops.

8 Bake in the preheated oven for 20–25 minutes, or until golden brown. Cool on a wire rack and serve.

4

6

7

Spiced Apple Doughnuts

INGREDIENTS

Makes 8

225 g/8 oz strong white flour
½ tsp salt
1½ tsp ground cinnamon
1 tsp easy-blend dried yeast
75 ml/3 fl oz warm milk
25 g/1 oz butter, melted
1 medium egg, beaten
oil, to deep-fry
4 tbsp caster sugar, to coat

For the filling:

2 small eating apples, peeled, cored
  and chopped
2 tsp soft light brown sugar
2 tsp lemon juice

1 Sift the flour, salt and 1 teaspoon of the cinnamon into a large bowl. Stir in the yeast and make a well in the centre.

2 Add the milk, butter and egg and mix to a soft dough. Knead on a lightly floured surface for 10 minutes, until smooth and elastic.

3 Divide the dough into eight pieces and shape each into a ball. Put on a floured baking sheet, cover with oiled clingfilm and leave in a warm place for 1 hour, or until doubled in size.

4 To make the filling, put the apples in a saucepan with the sugar, lemon juice and 3 tablespoons of water. Cover and simmer for about 10 minutes, then uncover and cook until fairly dry, stirring occasionally. Mash or blend in a food processor to a purée.

5 Pour enough oil into a deep-fat frying pan to come one-third of the way up the pan. Heat the oil to 180°C/350°F, then deep-fry the doughnuts for 1½–2 minutes on each side, until well browned.

6 Drain the doughnuts on kitchen paper, then roll in the caster sugar mixed with the remaining ½ teaspoon of ground cinnamon. Push a thick skewer into the centre to make a hole, then pipe in the apple filling. Serve warm or cold.

TASTY TIP

These doughnuts are also excellent when filled with pears. Simply replace the 2 apples with 2 pears and continue with the recipe. Look out for Comice pears as they are considered to be amongst the best on the market.

3   5   6

Maple, Pecan & Lemon Loaf

INGREDIENTS

Cuts into 12 slices

350 g/12 oz plain flour
1 tsp baking powder
175 g/6 oz butter, cubed
75 g/3 oz caster sugar
125 g/4 oz pecan nuts,
  roughly chopped
3 medium eggs
1 tbsp milk
finely grated rind of 1 lemon
5 tbsp maple syrup

For the icing:
75 g/3 oz icing sugar
1 tbsp lemon juice
25 g/1 oz pecans, roughly chopped

FOOD FACT

Maple syrup is made using the sap of the maple tree and has an intensely sweet, almost vanilla flavour. It is important to differentiate between the real thing and cheaper imitations which are maple-flavoured syrups, and contain artificial flavours.

1 Preheat the oven to 170°C/325°F/Gas Mark 3, 10 minutes before baking. Lightly oil and line the base of a 900 g/2 lb loaf tin with non-stick baking parchment.

2 Sift the flour and baking powder into a large bowl.

3 Rub in the butter until the mixture resembles fine breadcrumbs. Stir in the caster sugar and pecan nuts.

4 Beat the eggs together with the milk and lemon rind. Stir in the maple syrup. Add to the dry ingredients and gently stir in until mixed thoroughly to make a soft dropping consistency.

5 Spoon the mixture into the prepared tin and level the top with the back of a spoon. Bake on the middle shelf of the preheated oven for 50–60 minutes, or until the cake is well risen and lightly browned. If a skewer inserted into the centre comes out clean, then the cake is ready.

6 Leave the cake in the tin for about 10 minutes, then turn out and leave to cool on a wire rack. Carefully remove the lining paper.

7 Sift the icing sugar into a small bowl and stir in the lemon juice to make a smooth icing.

8 Drizzle the icing over the top of the loaf, then scatter with the chopped pecans. Leave to set, slice thickly and serve.

4

5

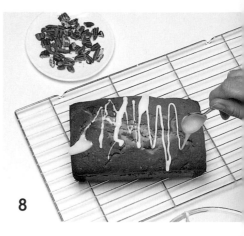

8

Moist Mincemeat Tea Loaf

INGREDIENTS

Cuts into 12 slices

225 g/8 oz self-raising flour
½ tsp ground mixed spice
125 g/4 oz cold butter, cubed
75 g/3 oz flaked almonds
25 g/1 oz glacé cherries, rinsed, dried
   and quartered
75 g/3 oz light muscovado sugar
2 medium eggs
250 g/9 oz prepared mincemeat
1 tsp lemon zest
2 tsp brandy or milk

FOOD FACT

Traditionally mincemeat contained cooked lean beef, but this is now omitted. Mince pies are now part of the Christmas fare in Britain. There are many different recipes, mostly containing suet, traditionally beef. With the increasing popularity of vegetarianism, however, vegetarian suet is now often used.

1 Preheat the oven to 180°C/350°F/Gas Mark 4, 10 minutes before cooking. Oil and line the base of a 900 g/2 lb loaf tin with non-stick baking paper.

2 Sift the flour and mixed spice into a large bowl. Add the butter and rub in until the mixture resembles breadcrumbs.

3 Reserve 2 tablespoons of the flaked almonds and stir in the rest with the glacé cherries and sugar.

4 Make a well in the centre of the dry ingredients. Lightly whisk the eggs, then stir in the mincemeat, lemon zest and brandy or milk.

5 Add the egg mixture and fold together until blended. Spoon into the prepared loaf tin, smooth the top with the back of a spoon, then sprinkle over the reserved flaked almonds.

6 Bake on the middle shelf of the preheated oven for 30 minutes. Cover with tinfoil to prevent the almonds browning too much. Bake for a further 30 minutes, or until well risen and a skewer inserted into the centre comes out clean.

7 Leave the tea loaf in the tin for 10 minutes before removing and cooling on a wire rack. Remove the lining paper, slice thickly and serve.

4

5

6

Marbled Chocolate & Orange Loaf

INGREDIENTS

Cuts into 6 slices

50 g/2 oz plain dark chocolate,
　broken into squares
125 g/4 oz butter, softened
125 g/4 oz caster sugar
zest of 1 orange
2 medium eggs, beaten
125 g/4 oz self-raising flour
2 tsp orange juice
1 tbsp cocoa powder, sifted

To finish:

1 tbsp icing sugar
1 tsp cocoa powder

TASTY TIP

To make a cream cheese icing for this cake, beat together 75 g/3 oz of cream cheese with 1–2 tablespoons of milk until smooth. Add a pinch of salt, 1 teaspoon of vanilla essence and 225 g/8 oz of icing sugar and mix well. Spread on top of the cake when cool.

1　Preheat the oven to 180°C/350°F/Gas Mark 4. Lightly oil a 450 g/1 lb loaf tin and line the base with a layer of non-stick baking paper.

2　Put the chocolate in a bowl over a saucepan of very hot water. Stir occasionally until melted. Remove and leave until just cool, but not starting to reset.

3　Meanwhile, cream together the butter, sugar and orange zest until pale and fluffy. Gradually add the beaten eggs, beating well after each addition.

4　Sift in the flour, add the orange juice and fold with a metal spoon or rubber spatula. Divide the mixture by half into two separate bowls. Gently fold the cocoa powder and chocolate into one half of the mixture.

5　Drop tablespoonfuls of each cake mixture into the prepared tin, alternating between the orange and chocolate mixtures. Briefly swirl the colours together with a knife to give a marbled effect.

6　Bake in the preheated oven for 40 minutes, or until firm and a fine skewer inserted into the centre comes out clean. Leave in the tin for 5 minutes, then turn out and cool on a wire rack. Carefully remove the lining paper.

7　Dust the cake with the icing sugar and then with the cocoa powder. Cut into thick slices and serve.

3

4

6

Fruity Apple Tea Bread

INGREDIENTS

Cuts into 12 slices

125 g/4 oz butter
125 g/4 oz soft light brown sugar
275 g/10 oz sultanas
150 ml/ ¼ pint apple juice
1 eating apple, peeled cored
   and chopped
2 medium eggs, beaten
275 g/10 oz plain flour
½ tsp ground cinnamon
½ tsp ground ginger
2 tsp bicarbonate of soda
curls of butter, to serve

To decorate:

1 eating apple, cored and sliced
1 tsp lemon juice
1 tbsp golden syrup, warmed

TASTY TIP

For an alcoholic version of this cake, soak the sultanas in brandy overnight before adding in step 2. To make the tea bread more moist in texture, add 1 grated carrot at the same time as the chopped apple in step 3.

1 Preheat the oven to 180°C/350°F/Gas Mark 4. Oil and line the base of a 900 g/2 lb loaf tin with non-stick baking paper.

2 Put the butter, sugar, sultanas and apple juice in a small saucepan. Heat gently, stirring occasionally until the butter has melted. Tip into a bowl and leave to cool.

3 Stir in the chopped apple and beaten eggs. Sift the flour, spices and bicarbonate of soda over the apple mixture.

4 Stir into the sultana mixture, spoon into the prepared loaf tin and smooth the top level with the back of a spoon.

5 Toss the apple slices in lemon juice and arrange on top.

6 Bake in the preheated oven for 50 minutes. Cover with tinfoil to prevent the top from browning too much.

7 Leave in the tin for 10 minutes before turning out to cool on to a wire rack.

8 Brush the top with golden syrup and leave to cool. Remove the lining paper, cut into thick slices and serve with curls of butter.

2

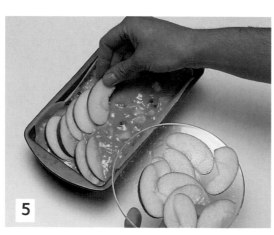
5

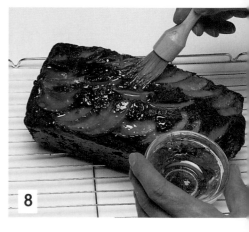
8

Buttery Passion Fruit Madeira Cake

INGREDIENTS

Cuts into 8–10 slices

210 g/7½ oz plain flour
1 tsp baking powder
175 g/6 oz unsalted butter, softened
250 g/9 oz caster sugar, plus 1 tsp
grated zest of 1 orange
1 tsp vanilla essence
3 medium eggs, beaten
2 tbsp milk
6 ripe passion fruits
50 g/2 oz icing sugar
icing sugar, to dust

FOOD FACT

Regardless of its name, Madeira cake does not actually originate from the Portuguese-owned island of Madeira. It is, in fact, a traditional English favourite, which acquired its name because the cake was often served with the fortified wine, Madeira.

1 Preheat the oven to 180°C/350°F/Gas Mark 4, 10 minutes before baking. Lightly oil and line the base of a 23 x 12.5 cm/9 x 5 inch loaf tin with greaseproof paper. Sift the flour and baking powder into a bowl and reserve.

2 Beat the butter, sugar, orange zest and vanilla essence until light and fluffy, then gradually beat in the eggs, 1 tablespoon at a time, beating well after each addition. If the mixture appears to curdle or separate, beat in a little of the flour mixture.

3 Fold in the flour mixture with the milk until just blended. Do not over mix. Spoon lightly into the prepared tin and smooth the top evenly. Sprinkle lightly with the teaspoon of caster sugar.

4 Bake in the preheated oven for 55 minutes, or until well risen and golden brown. Remove from the oven and leave to cool for 15–20 minutes. Turn the cake out of the tin and discard the lining paper.

5 Cut the passion fruits in half and scoop out the pulp into a sieve set over a bowl. Press the juice through using a rubber spatula or wooden spoon. Stir in the icing sugar and stir to dissolve, adding a little extra sugar if necessary.

6 Using a skewer, pierce holes all over the cake. Slowly spoon the passion fruit glaze over the cake and allow to seep in. Gently invert the cake on to a wire rack, then turn it back the right way up. Dust with icing sugar and cool completely. Serve the Madeira cake cold.

3

5

6

Step-by-Step, Practical Recipes Baking Breads: Tips & Hints

Helpful Hint

A good range of baking equipment, such as a pastry brush, used for glazing breads and buns, is essential. Perhaps most important is a good range of basic mixing cutlery: a wooden spoon for mixing, a spatula for transferring mixtures into baking tins, and a palette knife for easing breads and cakes out of their tins.

Tasty Tip

Unsalted butter is most commonly used in baking, especially for heavier sponge cakes such as Madeira Cake (see p46), as it gives a distinct, buttery flavour to your baking. Generally, butter and firm block margarine are the fats most often used in baking. Others fats can also be used, such as white vegetable fat, lard and oil. Low-fat spreads are not really very good for baking because they break down when cooked at high temperatures.

Food Fact

Flour comes in a range of varieties, each designed for a different job. Most of the recipes in this book recommend using strong flour, which is rich in gluten and is particularly good for making bread. You can also buy flour for coeliacs, which contains no gluten, while buckwheat, soya and chick pea flours are also available in many supermarkets.

Helpful Hint

More than any other type of cooking, when baking bread and cakes it is vital to accurately measure all your ingredients.

For example, the wrong amount of one ingredient can make bread too hard and difficult to eat. Equally important is that you set your oven at the correct heat.

Helpful Hint

Some of the recipes in this book require eggs. Eggs come in a variety of sizes and the size needed is shown in each recipe. As well as size, eggs come in a variety of types, such as free range or organic. It is really up to you which you prefer, though cost may influence your choice. The flavour of some eggs might be better than others, but there is very little nutritional difference. The key thing to look out for is the lion quality stamp, which guarantees eggs are safe to eat.

Helpful Hint

The rolling pin is perhaps one the most important kitchen implements for baking, so, if possible, invest in a good one. Ideally it should be long and thin, and heavy enough to roll the pastry out easily, but not so heavy that it is uncomfortable to use. When making flat breads, such as Focaccia (see p16), or scones (see p28), it is important to roll out the dough on a flat, lightly floured surface, to ensure the dough does not stick.

Helpful Hint

Baking trays, cake tins and loaf tins are essential for all cooks. Loaf tins are normally used for baking bread or tea loaves and generally come in two sizes: 450g/1 lb and 900 g/2 lb. Cakes tins come

in a variety of sizes, while baking sheets are really useful for baking a selection of scones or bagels. Also useful is a cooling rack, which allows your bread and cakes to cool more rapidly.

Tasty Tip

Italian breads, such as Focaccia (see p16), are almost a meal in themselves and make a great accompaniment to other Italian food such as antipasti, or are great just served as part of a sandwich.

Food Fact

Three types of yeast are available in the shops: fresh yeast, which can now be bought from the bakery in many supermarkets, dried yeast, which is available in tins, and quick-acting yeast, which comes in packets. Fresh yeast should only be bought in small quantities, while dried yeast can be stored for up to six months. Quick-acting yeast cuts down the bread-making time and can be added straight to the flour without having to be activated.

Helpful Hint

To ensure a loaf, such as a Maple, Pecan & Lemon Loaf (see p38), is thoroughly cooked, remove it from the oven and insert a clean skewer into the middle. Leave it for 30 seconds and then remove. If the cake is completely clean then the cake is cooked; if there is a little mixture left on the skewer, then you need to return it to the oven for a few minutes.

First published in 2012 by
FLAME TREE PUBLISHING LTD
Crabtree Hall, Crabtree Lane, Fulham,
London, SW6 6TY, United Kingdom
www.flametreepublishing.com

NOTE: Recipes using uncooked eggs should be avoided by infants, the elderly, pregnant women and anyone suffering from an illness.

18 17 16 15 14 13 12   10 9 8 7 6 5 4 3 2 1

ISBN: 978-0-85775-616-9

ACKNOWLEDGEMENTS: Authors: Catherine Atkinson, Juliet Barker, Gina Steer, Vicki Smallwood, Carol Tennant, Mari Mererid Williams, Elizabeth Wolf-Cohen and Simone Wright. Photography: Colin Bowling, Paul Forrester and Stephen Brayne. Home Economists and Stylists: Jacqueline Bellefontaine, Mandy Phipps, Vicki Smallwood and Penny Stephens. All props supplied by Barbara Stewart at Surfaces. Publisher and Creative Director: Nick Wells. Editorial: Catherine Taylor, Sarah Goulding, Marcus Hardie, Gina Steer and Karen Fitzpatrick. Design and Production: Chris Herbert, Mike Spender, Colin Rudderham and Helen Wall.